DIGITAL THREADS

COMPANION WORKBOOK

The Small Business and
Entrepreneur Playbook for
Digital First Marketing

NEAL SCHAFFER

Published by PDCA Social
https://nealschaffer.com

ISBN 979-8-9906127-0-9 (eBook)
ISBN 979-8-9906127-1-6 (paperback)
ISBN 979-8-9906127-2-3 (audio)

First Edition: May 2024

Disclaimer: This workbook is intended to provide educational information on the subjects discussed. It is sold with the understanding that the author and publisher are not engaged in rendering legal, accounting, or other professional services. If legal advice or other expert assistance is required, the services of a competent professional should be sought.

The strategies, tips, and tools discussed in this book are based on the author's personal experience and knowledge in the field of digital marketing. They are not intended to guarantee that readers will achieve the same or similar results. The author and publisher disclaim any warranties (express or implied), merchantability, or fitness for any particular purpose. The author and publisher shall in no event be held liable for any loss or other damages, including but not limited to special, incidental, consequential, or other damages.

As always with anything in business and life, your mileage may vary. What works for one may not work for all. Take what you can use, adapt it to your own context, and always test and refine for the best results in your specific situation.

Remember, the digital landscape is ever evolving. While the strategies and insights shared in this workbook are based on the latest trends and practices at the time of writing, the world of digital marketing is always changing. Keep learning, stay flexible, and adapt to new developments to stay ahead in the game.

THANK YOU FOR READING DIGITAL THREADS!

This is the companion workbook to Digital Threads, which I hope you have finished reading by now. I appreciate any feedback and would love to hear what you thought about Digital Threads.

Your input is essential to help make Digital Threads, this companion workbook, and my future books even better to serve more people.

Please take a minute now to leave a review on Amazon letting me know what you thought of the book:

nealschaffer.com/digitalthreadsreview

I cannot thank you enough! If you used a non-recognizable name, please send me a screenshot to neal@nealschaffer.com so that I can personally thank you!

- Neal Schaffer

P.S. If you haven't bought Digital Threads yet, you can find it here:

nealschaffer.com/digitalthreads

INTRODUCTION TO THIS WORKBOOK

This workbook is a companion workbook to my *Digital Threads* book, available in all formats everywhere you purchase (or borrow) a book.

The inspiration for creating this workbook, a first for me even though this is my fifth book, comes from my teaching executives at various universities. In my early teaching days, a program director gave me some invaluable advice: Instead of my speaking all the time and answering questions here and there, why not try to include exercises throughout the lesson that enable students to put into practice what I am teaching? When I started doing that, I could see the magic happen. After learning about the "I Do, We Do, You Do" teaching strategy, I further embraced the development of engaging in classroom exercises. This workbook extends these concepts, aiming to help you internalize what I teach in *Digital Threads* by having you do the work that you can apply to your unique business strategy.

I have done my best to develop activities for each chapter to ensure balance among the various topics covered in *Digital Threads*. Additionally, I have included a summary of the topics covered in each chapter, divided into parts, to help refresh your memory. This is no way a substitution for reading *Digital Threads* in its entirety, so please make sure you finish reading the book before starting the first exercise here to get the most out of this workbook.

If you enjoyed this workbook and have ideas for other exercises to include, or just wanted to share your feedback after going through some or all the exercises, I would love to hear from you. Please email me: neal@nealschaffer.com

CONTENTS

INTRODUCTION

Chapter One: The New Digital Landscape of Today

Summary of Main Points:

1. **Evolving Marketing Landscape**: The necessity for businesses to continuously adapt their strategies to changing consumer habits and technological advancements.

2. **Acceleration of Digital Adoption**: The COVID-19 pandemic has fast-tracked the shift towards a digital economy, accelerating the change in how consumers work, shop, and interact.

3. **Opportunities and Challenges**: The digital era offers direct communication and sales channels but requires authenticity and engagement to overcome consumer skepticism.

4. **Integration of Traditional and Digital Marketing**: While digital strategies are paramount, the foundational principles of marketing remain relevant.

Chapter Two: The New Marketing Infrastructure of Today

Summary of Main Points:

1. **Digital Marketing Landscape**: Digital marketing provides you with a plethora of options, including social media, communication platforms, and traditional channels like search and email.

2. **Marketing Funnel Adaptation**: The adaptation of the traditional AIDA marketing funnel to digital, the need for multiple touchpoints and the importance of building trust.

3. **Digital Marketing Containers**: I introduce the concept of "containers" to simplify digital marketing into manageable channels, focusing on websites, search engines, email marketing, content marketing, social media marketing, and influencer marketing.

4. **SES Framework**: A streamlined approach focusing on Search, Email, and Social as the core pillars of a digital marketing strategy, each having unique roles in building relationships with customers and navigating the digital marketing funnel.

1.1 | How Much Do You Buy Online?

This exercise is intended to remind you how the digital transformation has influenced our purchasing behavior, further demonstrating the importance of a digital first marketing strategy.

1. Reflect on your business and personal expenditures online now versus pre-pandemic (5 years ago) and compare to 20 years ago. Document the changes in spending habits.
2. Identify new categories of personal and business expenses that have shifted to online in recent years that weren't previously considered.
3. Analyze how this shift has impacted your buying habits, both personally as well as for your business.

	What do you Buy In-Person?	What Do You Buy Online?	What Online Subscription Services Do You Use?
Now			
5 Years Ago			
20 Years Ago			

How has this shift impacted your buying habits?

_____

_____

_____

_____

1.2 │ How Much Research Do You Do Online?

This exercise will remind you how much you use the Internet to do research before making a purchase, proving the importance of a digital first marketing strategy to appear online when your target customer is searching for a solution that you can provide.

1. Assess how often you conduct online research before making buying decisions, whether it is product research for personal consumption or vendor selection and market analysis for business purposes.
2. Identify the digital platforms (e.g., search engines, social media, review sites, blogs) you primarily use for your research.
3. Evaluate the influence of digital research on how you make purchases and how it has evolved.

Where You Research	Percentage
Online	
Visit Physical Store	
Ask Friends and Family (Offline)	
Read Magazines and Newspapers	
Other:	

Platform Category	Use for what decisions?
Amazon	
Other Retail Websites (Walmart, Target, etc.)	
Brand Websites	
Search Engines (Google, etc.)	
Social Media (TikTok, Instagram, YouTube, etc.)	
Consumer Reviews (Yelp, Trustpilot, TripAdvisor, etc.)	
Price Comparison Websites (Shopzilla, Bizrate, Google Shopping, Kayak, etc.)	
Ask Your Friend/Family Online	
Ask Your Friend/Family Offline	
Influence of Digital Research:	

2.1 | Google's Zero Moment of Truth

Recall Google's ZMOT definition: the moment when a consumer starts researching a product before the actual purchase.

Reflect on a personal experience where you spent time researching before a purchase. What did you purchase and how much research did you do?

List the different touchpoints (reviews, social media, brand websites, etc.) encountered during your research.

☐ Amazon ☐ Retailer Website ☐ Brand Website ☐ Search Engine

☐ YouTube ☐ Facebook ☐ TikTok ☐ Instagram

☐ Twitter/X ☐ Pinterest ☐ Consumer Review Websites ☐ Price Comparison Websites

☐ Friend/Family Online ☐ Friends/Family Offline ☐ Saw Product in Store ☐ Saw TV Ad

☐ Heard Radio Ad ☐ Saw Billboard ☐ Saw in Newspaper/Magazine ☐ Other

Reflect on how many touchpoints it took to convert you and where they occurred:

_____

_____

_____

_____

_____

_____

_____

_____

2.2 | Internalizing the AIDA Funnel

1. Analyze how your company moves prospects through the Awareness, Interest, Desire, Action (AIDA) funnel.
2. Cite specific marketing activities your company uses at each stage of the funnel.
3. Evaluate the effectiveness of these activities and identify any gaps or misalignments.

Awareness

How will people get to know about your brand/product/service?

Interest

How will you get potential customers interested in learning more about your product/service?

Desire

How will you get potential customers to prefer your product/service as the best solution to their problem?

Action

How will you get potential customers to commit and purchase your product/service?

2.3 | Analyzing the 6 Marketing Containers

1. Fill in the table for each of the six marketing containers mentioned in the chapter (e.g., websites, search engines, email marketing, content marketing, social media marketing, influencer marketing).
2. Assess the ROI from each container and identify any gaps or misalignments in spending versus results.

Container Name	# of Internal Resources	Non-Personnel Expenses	Perceived Results
Websites			
Search Engines			
Email Marketing			
Content Marketing			
Social Media Marketing			
Influencer Marketing			

Assess ROI	

2.4 | Analyzing the SES Framework

1. Analyze your current marketing activities against the SES framework to ensure balanced investment across search, email, and social media marketing.
2. Assess the ROI from each container and identify any gaps or misalignments in spending versus results.

	# of Internal Resources	Non-Personnel Expenses	Perceived Results
Search			
Email			
Social Media			
Balanced Investment – Why/Why Not?			

_____

_____

_____

Assess ROI

_____

_____

_____

_____

PART ONE – RETINKING IT ALL

Chapter Three – RETHINK SEARCH

Summary of Main Points:

1. **Expanded Definition of Search**: Search engines are any platform where people discover content, including social media and e-commerce sites in addition to traditional search engines.

2. **Long-term Discoverability**: I recommend creating content with a longer shelf-life, such as blogs, podcasts, and YouTube videos, to ensure sustained visibility.

3. **Evergreen Content**: The importance of creating content that remains relevant and valuable regardless of the season or trends.

4. **Search Demand and Intent**: The importance of aligning content with what people are searching for, including understanding the intent behind search queries.

5. **Beyond Traditional Search Engines**: The nuances of various platforms' algorithms, such as Amazon and YouTube, and their impact on content discoverability.

Chapter Four - RETHINK EMAIL

Summary of Main Points:

1. **Enduring Power of Email**: Despite newer marketing channels, email remains highly effective due to its high ROI and direct engagement with audiences.

2. **Value and Personalization**: Email is essential for deepening relationships, providing value, and maintaining subscriber interest and trust through personalization.

3. **Segmentation and Targeting**: Critical for tailoring messages to subscriber preferences, enhancing engagement, and increasing conversions.

4. **Storytelling and Engagement**: Use storytelling to keep subscribers interested over time, which fosters a sense of connection and trust.

5. **List Management and Automation**: Pruning inactive subscribers and leveraging automation to maintain a healthy, engaged email list and automate the customer journey.

Chapter Five - RETHINK SOCIAL MEDIA

Summary of Main Points:

1. **Social Media's True Purpose**: Focus on connection and engagement with people, not direct sales pitches or corporate messaging.

2. **Authentic Engagement**: The importance of genuine interactions over promotional content to build trust and community.

3. **Influence and Content Quality**: Creating quality content and leveraging influencers who share brand values are more effective activities than focusing on follower counts.

4. **Consistency and Algorithm Understanding**: Consistent content creation tailored to platform algorithms will help increase audience engagement.

5. **Strategic Experimentation**: View social media marketing strategy as an ongoing experiment to refine approaches based on what engages the audience.

3.1 | Content Discoverability Worksheet

1. **List Platforms:** Write down 3 strategic platforms where you publish content (e.g., blog, podcast, YouTube, LinkedIn, Facebook, Instagram, etc.).
2. **Rate Discoverability:** Next to each content platform, rate how discoverable your content is on a scale of 1 - 10, with 10 being the most visible.
3. **Explain Ratings:** Provide reasons for your ratings, considering the platform's algorithm, audience engagement, and content lifespan.
4. **Reflect on Production:** Assess the amount and type of content you produce, focusing on its potential for discoverability. Brainstorm strategies to increase discoverability.

Content Platform

	1 2 3 4 5 6 7 8 9 10
	Explain your rating:
	What is your quantity of content?

	1 2 3 4 5 6 7 8 9 10
	Explain your rating:
	What is your quantity of content?

	1 2 3 4 5 6 7 8 9 10
	Explain your rating:
	What is your quantity of content?

Strategies to increase discoverability:

3.2 | Timeless Treasure Hunt: The Evergreen Content Evaluation

1. Think of the most common questions your business receives. List the top 10 questions.
2. Reflect on whether these questions were relevant 5 years ago and if they will remain relevant 5 years into the future.
3. Based on this reflection, rate how evergreen the content answering these questions would be on a scale from 1 to 10.
4. Consider creating content that addresses these questions if it aligns with a high evergreen score, indicating long-term value and relevance.

	Relevance		
Common Questions	**5 Years Ago**	**Next 5 Years**	**Rating**
	Yes No	Yes No	1 2 3 4 5 6 7 8 9 10
	Yes No	Yes No	1 2 3 4 5 6 7 8 9 10
	Yes No	Yes No	1 2 3 4 5 6 7 8 9 10
	Yes No	Yes No	1 2 3 4 5 6 7 8 9 10
	Yes No	Yes No	1 2 3 4 5 6 7 8 9 10
	Yes No	Yes No	1 2 3 4 5 6 7 8 9 10
	Yes No	Yes No	1 2 3 4 5 6 7 8 9 10
	Yes No	Yes No	1 2 3 4 5 6 7 8 9 10
	Yes No	Yes No	1 2 3 4 5 6 7 8 9 10
	Yes No	Yes No	1 2 3 4 5 6 7 8 9 10

Reflect on your evergreen content action plan: _____

_____

_____

_____

3.3 | Keyword Quest: Intent Exploration

1. Identify 10 keywords that you believe your ideal customer might use to find your product or service.
2. Conduct searches for each keyword in the private/incognito mode of your preferred search engine and analyze the content that appears at or near the top of the organic search results.
3. Note any surprises or discrepancies between your expectations and the actual search results.
4. Reflect on the search intent behind each keyword and how well your content aligns with this intent.
5. Adjust your content strategy based on your findings to better meet the needs and intents of your target audience.

Keywords	What appears in your search?	What surprised you with your search?	How are you going to adjust?

Reflect on what content strategy adjustments you should make: _____

_____

_____

_____

4.1 | Value-Driven Email Design

1. **Core Value Identification:** Identify the core value your brand offers to its customers. This is the foundation of your email message.
2. **Subject Line Creation:** Craft a compelling subject line that captures the essence of the email's value.
3. **Email Drafting:** Draft an email that communicates your brand's core value. Make sure it addresses your audience's needs or interests.
4. **Call-to-Action Integration:** Decide on a specific action you want your readers to take. Integrate a call-to-action that clearly states this.

Core Value:	
Subject Line:	
Email Draft:	
Call to Action:	

4.2 | Audience Segmentation Exercise

Current State	Future Planning
Part 1: Current Segmentation Analysis 1. Review how your email list is currently segmented. 2. Assess the effectiveness of these segments in achieving targeted communication and engagement.	**Part 2: Advanced Segmentation Planning** 1. Identify additional criteria for deeper segmentation, such as interests, purchase behaviors, and engagement levels. 2. Outline how you would communicate differently with each segment to better meet their needs.
Current Segmentation:	New Segments:
Effectiveness:	What to Communicate to Who:

4.3 | Storytelling That Sells

Write an email that incorporates storytelling to strengthen connections with subscribers, using elements that highlight your brand's essence, customer success, or unique processes.

"Your currency is storytelling. People love stories."

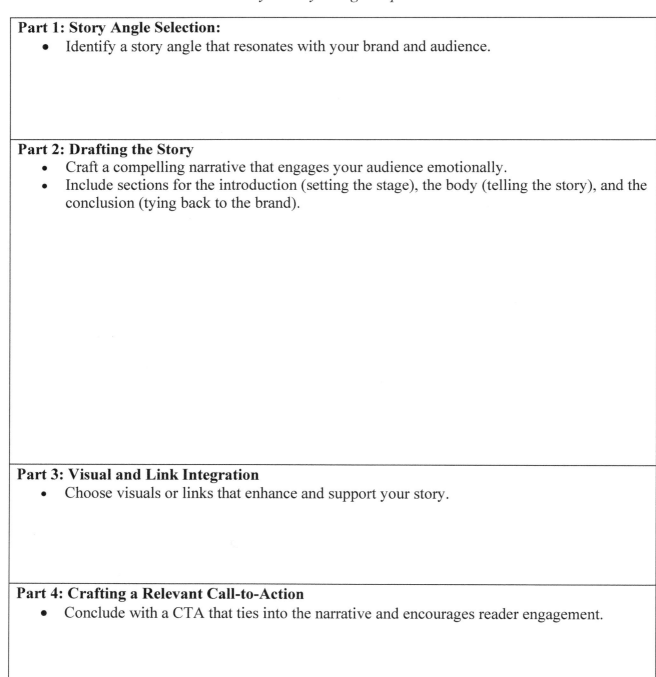

Part 1: Story Angle Selection:
- Identify a story angle that resonates with your brand and audience.

Part 2: Drafting the Story
- Craft a compelling narrative that engages your audience emotionally.
- Include sections for the introduction (setting the stage), the body (telling the story), and the conclusion (tying back to the brand).

Part 3: Visual and Link Integration
- Choose visuals or links that enhance and support your story.

Part 4: Crafting a Relevant Call-to-Action
- Conclude with a CTA that ties into the narrative and encourages reader engagement.

4.4 | Clean List, Clear Strategy

1. Perform an analysis of your email list to identify inactive subscribers and develop a strategy that details removal criteria for their re-engagement or removal, ensuring the health of the list.

Removal Criteria 1	Removal Criteria 2

Removal Criteria 3	Removal Criteria 4

2. Create a re-engagement email that appeals to their interests or offers an incentive for feedback.

_____

_____

_____

_____

_____

_____

3. Determine what removal steps to take after sending how many emails over the course of how many days.

Removal Step 1	Date

Removal Step 2	Date:

Removal Step 3	Date:

5.1 | How Much Time Do You Spend in Social Media?

Measuring how much time you spend in social media will help you recognize its strategic importance.

Part 1: Tracking Social Media Use
Use your device's tracking feature, Screen Time (iOS) or Digital Wellbeing (Android), monitor and record your daily social media app usage. Record your daily average usage over the last week.

Part 2: Pre-Social Media Reflection
Think back to your daily routine before social media. How did you spend your leisure time?

Part 3: Reflective Writing
Reflect on your tracked social media usage and compare it to your previous leisure activities. Consider the impact of social media on your daily life.

	Facebook	TikTok	Instagram	YouTube	LinkedIn	Twitter/X	Pinterest
Social Media Use							

Other:

Pre-Social Media Reflection

Reflective Writing

5.2 | The Consistency Challenge

Develop a habit of consistent content creation to enhance engagement on social media. Choose which social network(s) and days of the week you will consistently post.

	Facebook		Instagram		YouTube		LinkedIn
	TikTok		Pinterest		X/Twitter		Other:

	Sunday		Monday		Tuesday		Wednesday
	Thursday		Friday		Saturday		

Brainstorm and list the first 8 topics or themes you intend to cover in your posts.

I pledge to maintain my posting schedule for 8 consecutive weeks.

Signature: _____

Week 1 Date(s): Topic(s):	Week 2 Date(s): Topic(s):	Week 3 Date(s): Topic(s):	Week 4 Date(s): Topic(s):
Week 5 Date(s): Topic(s):	Week 6 Date(s): Topic(s):	Week 7 Date(s): Topic(s):	Week 8 Date(s): Topic(s):

After completing the 8 weeks, reflect on the process and reevaluate the impact on your social media engagement metrics based on both social network and topic or theme.

5.3 | Adapt & Expand Engagement

Part 1: Content Selection

Choose a single piece of content you plan to adapt. Provide a brief description of the content.

Part 2: Platform Adaptation

1. Modify the selected content for two different social media platforms. Focus on adjusting the format, caption, and use of hashtags to align with each platform's preferences and audience.
2. Document the specific changes made for each platform and explain why these adjustments were necessary.
3. After posting, analyze and compare the engagement received on both platforms.

Platform 1: _____　　　Platform 2: _____

Detail the adaptations made for each platform.	
Modifications and the rationale behind each social platform	
After posting, analyze and compare the engagement received on both platforms.	

5.4 | Unlocking Social Media Content Success

Evaluate the performance of your social media content to identify successful strategies.

Step 1: Performance Review
- Examine the analytics or manually review the performance of your last 25 social media posts on your most strategic social network. Make note of your top-performing posts in the space below:

_____

_____

Step 2: Characteristics of Success
- Identify the common features of your top-performing posts.

Content Format	Content Length	Caption	Content Quality	Content Topic
Call to Action	Hashtags Used	Account/Location tagged	Day of the Week	Time of Day
Other:				

Step 3: Trend Analysis
- Analyze your findings to uncover trends and patterns associated with high engagement levels.

_____

_____

Step 4: Strategic Planning
- Based on your analysis, outline a strategy for future content that leverages the insights gained from your top-performing posts.

_____

_____

PART TWO – BEGIN (AGAIN)

Chapter Six - BE FOUND

Summary of Main Points:

1. **Content as Capital**: Content's value in building asset, authority and digital presence.

2. **Discoverability in Search Engines**: The importance of being found through search engines and creating content strategically for this purpose.

3. **Role of Blogs**: A blog has a strategic role in gaining visibility and establishing authority online.

4. **Search Engine Algorithms**: Search engines prioritize helpful content and have frequent algorithm updates in order to serve the best content to each search query.

5. **Helpful Content**: The importance of creating content that is genuinely useful to a reader.

6. **Keyword Strategy**: The process of selecting and targeting keywords to enhance discoverability and authority in a specific field.

7. **Library of Content**: The concept of building a comprehensive collection of content that showcases expertise and builds trust.

Chapter Seven - BE IN TOUCH

Summary of Main Points:

1. **Value of Giving Away Content**: Sharing valuable content is crucial for attracting potential customers and building trust.

2. **Email Strategy**: Email serves as a medium to continue conversation with potential customers, moving them further down the sales funnel.

3. **Building Lead Magnets**: Lead magnets are designed to capture the attention and contact details of potential customers by offering them something valuable.

4. **Targeting and Customization**: Understanding the target audience is key to creating effective lead magnets that resonate and convert.

Chapter Eight - BE SEEN

Summary of Main Points:

1. **Evolution of Social Media:** How social media has transformed, particularly post-pandemic, becoming a primary space for marketing due to its vast user engagement.

2. **Challenges for Businesses:** With the rise of social media, businesses face the challenge of cutting through the noise due to algorithm changes and the need for paid promotion.

3. **Platform Authentic Content:** Create content that is genuine and tailored to each platform's unique format and audience preferences.

4. **Engagement Over Promotion:** The shift from direct promotion to engaging content that resonates with and adds value to the audience.

5. **Adapting to Algorithms:** Understanding and adapting to platform algorithms is crucial for content visibility and engagement.

6. **Strategic Content Repurposing:** Repurpose content across platforms in a way that remains authentic and engaging to each audience.

6.1 | Rank Up with Blogs

1. Refer to the 10 keywords identified in Exercise 3.3 (Keyword Quest: Intent Exploration, page 19).
2. Conduct a search for each of the 5 most strategic keywords and analyze the top 20 search results.
3. For each keyword, list how many blog posts appear in the top 20 results.
4. Note what these blog posts are about and which websites host them.
5. Reflect on the diversity of websites and relevance of topics to your business covered in these posts.

Keyword	How Many of the Top 20 are Blogs?	Titles of Blog Posts	Domain Name of Blog

Reflect on the relevance of the blog post topics to your business. Is there a chance for you to offer helpful advice to rank here as well?

_____

_____

_____

_____

_____

6.2 | Timeless vs. Timely Content

1. For the 5 keywords identified in the previous exercise, examine the top 20 search results for their publication dates.
2. Record the publication year, where available, for each of the 20 posts across the 5 keywords.
3. Identify trends in the publication dates - are they recent, older, or a mix?
4. Select the oldest ranking post for each keyword and evaluate its content for outdated information.
5. Consider how you could update or improve upon this content in your own blog posts.

	Keyword 1	Keyword 2	Keyword 3	Keyword 4	Keyword 5
1					
2					
3					
4					
5					
6					
7					
8					
9					
10					
11					
12					
13					
14					
15					
16					
17					
18					
19					
20					

6.3 | How Helpful is Your Content

1. Compare the #1 and #20 ranked search results for each of your 5 keywords.
2. Identify what makes the #1 ranked content more helpful than the #20 ranked content, considering aspects like content depth, user experience, and interactive elements.
3. Reflect on how you can apply these insights to improve the helpfulness of your own content.

Keyword:

#1 Ranked Blog Post Title	Analyze and note the differences	What can I do with this information?
#20 Ranked Blog Post Title		

Keyword:

#1 Ranked Blog Post Title	Analyze and note the differences	What can I do with this information?
#20 Ranked Blog Post Title		

Keyword:

#1 Ranked Blog Post Title	Analyze and note the differences	What can I do with this information?
#20 Ranked Blog Post Title		

Keyword:

#1 Ranked Blog Post Title	Analyze and note the differences	What can I do with this information?
#20 Ranked Blog Post Title		

Keyword:

#1 Ranked Blog Post Title	Analyze and note the differences	What can I do with this information?
#20 Ranked Blog Post Title		

6.4 │ Planning Your Library of Content

1. Use an SEO tool (see the Tools Glossary for my recommendations) to research one anchor keyword related to your business.
2. Generate a list of 52 unique and relevant keyword variations based on search intent.
3. For each keyword, enter the information in the table below.
4. Strategize your content creation starting with the least competitive keywords, but also consider your own approach to prioritization.

Week #	Keyword	Check Search Intent	Search Demand	Keyword Competition	Potential Blog Title	Priority
1		☐				
2		☐				
3		☐				
4		☐				
5		☐				
6		☐				
7		☐				
8		☐				
9		☐				
10		☐				
11		☐				
12		☐				
13		☐				
14		☐				
15		☐				
16		☐				
17		☐				
18		☐				
19		☐				
20		☐				
21		☐				
22		☐				

Week #	Keyword	Check Search Intent	Search Demand	Keyword Competition	Potential Blog Title	Priority
23		☐				
24		☐				
25		☐				
26		☐				
27		☐				
28		☐				
29		☐				
30		☐				
31		☐				
32		☐				
33		☐				
34		☐				
35		☐				
36		☐				
37		☐				
38		☐				
39		☐				
40		☐				
41		☐				
42		☐				
43		☐				
44		☐				
45		☐				
46		☐				
47		☐				
48		☐				
49		☐				
50		☐				
51		☐				
52		☐				

7.1 | Creating Your Ideal Lead Magnet

Brainstorm and plan four distinct lead magnet ideas tailored to your business needs, focusing on attracting and providing value to your target customers.

Circle four from the list below you have decided to create and fill in the table below:

In-Person Consultation	Discounted Service	Coupon	Exclusive Access	Report or White Paper
E-Book	Guides	Resource List	Webinar	Video Training
Virtual Summit	Email Course	Online Challenge	Free Online Course	Checklist or Cheat Sheet
Workbook	Quiz/Survey	Test	Assessment	Giveaway
Contests	Templates	Case Studies	Infographic	Free Trial

Lead Magnet	1.	2.	3.	4.
Why Is It Valuable to Potential Customers?				
Content Creation				
Delivery Mechanism				
Promotion Strategy				

8.1 | Analyze the Algorithm

1. Choose four social networks to analyze (e.g., Facebook, Instagram, Twitter, LinkedIn).
2. Scroll through the first 20 posts in your feed and categorize each post into one of the three listed categories.
3. Record the number of each type in the table.

	Social Network			
Organic Content from People				
Ads				
Organic Content from Businesses				

Reflect on what you saw:
- Did it confirm what you thought you would see?
- Did it confirm the differences between algorithms between each platform? (more ads on some, more organic business content, etc.)
- Do you feel your content has a good chance to rank in the algorithm? Why or why not?

_____

_____

_____

_____

_____

_____

8.2 | Adapting to Platform Authentic Content

1. Select a blog post you have written or find one that interests you to repurpose.
2. Break down the key points or sections of the blog post. Identify the main idea, supporting points, interesting facts, quotes, or statistics.
3. Repurpose the content into the following formats: Long-form Text with an Image (for LinkedIn or Facebook), Thread (for Twitter or Threads), Carousel Image (for LinkedIn, Facebook, or Instagram) Shortform Video (TikTok, Instagram Reels and/or YouTube Shorts)

Blog Post Title	
Key Points	
Supporting Points	
Interesting Facts, Quotes or Statistics	

Using the information from above, start to plan out the steps you will take to create each of these formats.

Long-form Text with an Image	
Thread	
Carousel Image	
Shortform Video	

8.3 | Reset and Reconnaissance

Creating a second profile on social media platforms like Instagram, TikTok or YouTube can help you better understand the content that your target audience is consuming to be more effective with your own content creation. Let's learn how.

Instagram	TikTok	YouTube
1. Open the Instagram app and go to your profile. 2. Tap on the hamburger menu (three lines) in the top right corner, then select 'Settings'. 3. Scroll down to 'Add Account' and tap on 'Create New Account'. 4. Follow the on-screen instructions to choose a username and complete the setup. 5. Once the account is created, you can switch between your accounts by tapping your username at the top of your profile. 6. To Begin: Start by searching for profiles like the theme or niche you are interested in. Follow them and engage with their content to start building your network.	1. Open the TikTok app and go to your profile. 2. Tap on the three dots in the top right corner to access 'Settings and Privacy'. 3. Scroll down to 'Switch Account', then tap on '+ Add account'. 4. Choose the method you wish to sign up with and follow the prompts to set up your new account. 5. To Begin: Use the search function to find content creators or hashtags that align with your new account's focus. Engaging with this content can help refine your feed and suggest connections.	1. Sign in to YouTube with your Google account. 2. Click on your profile icon in the top right corner, then select 'Switch account'. 3. Click on 'Add account' and sign in with another Google account or create a new one. 4. Once signed in, click on your profile icon again, then 'Your channel' and follow the prompts to create a new channel. 5. To Begin: Start by searching for channels that inspire you or are similar to what you want to create. Subscribe and interact with their content to get a feel for the community and trends.

It's time to search...

- Engage with content by "liking" posts that:
    1. Appeal to your target audience.
    2. Represent high-quality content you find worth emulating.
- Begin following users after you've liked several of their posts.
- This approach will:
    1. Help you understand influential content creators in your target market.
    2. Provide insights into the content your target audience engages with.
    3. Serve as inspiration for your own content creation.

Neal Schaffer

PART THREE – OPTIMIZE

Chapter Nine - BUILD CONNECTIONS

Summary of Main Points:

1. **Importance of Backlinks**: Backlinks are crucial for enhancing domain authority and improving search engine rankings.

2. **Quality over Quantity**: The importance of acquiring relevant and authoritative backlinks rather than focusing on sheer volume.

3. **Building Relationships**: Backlink generation is an opportunity to build valuable relationships within the digital marketing community.

4. **Practical Backlink Strategies**: There are a variety of strategies for acquiring backlinks, such as leveraging HARO and engaging in guest blogging.

Chapter Ten - BUILD PATHS

Summary of Main Points:

1. **Active Engagement**: Regular communication with contacts is crucial for keeping the relationship alive and preventing disinterest.

2. **Value of Storytelling**: Utilizing storytelling in email marketing helps in connecting with the audience on a personal level, making your brand memorable.

3. **Email Marketing Strategy**: A structured approach to email marketing is recommended, focusing on building relationships rather than just sending promotions.

4. **Communication Pathways**: There are seven primary pathways to engage with email subscribers, each serving a unique purpose in the marketing strategy.

Chapter Eleven - BUILD VISIBILITY

Summary of Main Points:

1. **Leveraging UGC for Authenticity:** UGC fosters a genuine connection between brands and their audience, enhancing consumer trust and engagement.

2. **Cost-Effective Content Strategy:** Utilizing UGC reduces the need for expensive content production, offering a budget-friendly approach to maintaining an active online presence.

3. **Enhanced Engagement through UGC:** UGC not only increases social media activity but also boosts overall engagement and sales by providing relatable and persuasive content.

4. **Strategies to Encourage UGC:** These strategies include contests, branded hashtags, and influencer partnerships, all which help to effectively generate and capitalize on user content.

9.1 | Backlink Audit

1. **Visit Ahref's Website Authority Checker:** Go to https://ahrefs.com/website-authority-checker/.
2. **Enter Your Website URL (yourdomain.com):** Start by checking your own site's home page to get your domain rating and the total number of websites that link to you.
3. **Check Competitor Websites:** List 10 competitors and repeat the process for each to gather their domain rating and number of websites that link to them.

Site Name	Domain Rating	Number of Linking Websites
Your Site		
Competitor 1		
Competitor 2		
Competitor 3		
Competitor 4		
Competitor 5		
Competitor 6		
Competitor 7		
Competitor 8		
Competitor 9		
Competitor 10		

Backlink Comparative Analysis

How does your domain compare with the competition?
What correlations do you see between domain rating and number of backlinks?

9.2 | Directory Backlink Boost

1. Use SEO tools or search Google for "business directories and listing sites list" and look for titles such as "XX Best Online Business Directories & Listing Sites and "Top XX Free Business Listing Sites" to identify industry-specific and local business directories where your competitors are listed.
2. Scan for 5 directories where your company is not already listed but is relevant and register.

Directory Name:	Competitor Presence:	
Relevance	Domain Rating:	Registered? ☐Yes ☐No
Directory Name:	Competitor Presence:	
Relevance	Domain Rating:	Registered? ☐Yes ☐No
Directory Name:	Competitor Presence:	
Relevance	Domain Rating:	Registered? ☐Yes ☐No
Directory Name:	Competitor Presence:	
Relevance	Domain Rating:	Registered? ☐Yes ☐No
Directory Name:	Competitor Presence:	
Relevance	Domain Rating:	Registered? ☐Yes ☐No

9.3 | The Write for Us Lottery

1. Use search engines to find guest blogging opportunities by typing "[industry name] blogs looking for guest posts" or "write for us + [industry name]".
2. Aim to gather information on at least 5 different blogs or websites that accept guest posts and enter the information below:

Domain Name	Domain Rating	Relevant Topics Welcome	Word Count Guidance	Links Allowed (if mentioned)

Use the following to project manage these five guest blog posts.

Domain Name	Submitted ☐	Date	Expected Publication Date:	Published ☐
URL of Published Post			Specific Links Back to Your Domain	
Domain Name	Submitted ☐	Date	Expected Publication Date:	Published ☐
URL of Published Post			Specific Links Back to Your Domain	
Domain Name	Submitted ☐	Date	Expected Publication Date:	Published ☐
URL of Published Post			Specific Links Back to Your Domain	
Domain Name	Submitted ☐	Date	Expected Publication Date:	Published ☐
URL of Published Post			Specific Links Back to Your Domain	
Domain Name	Submitted ☐	Date	Expected Publication Date:	Published ☐
URL of Published Post			Specific Links Back to Your Domain	

9.4 | Pitch Perfect Blogging

Create a compelling outreach email for guest post opportunities by leveraging and customizing existing successful templates.

Research Phase:

- Perform a Google search for "guest post outreach email" to find popular and effective email templates used for guest blogging outreach.
- Review various templates and select one that resonates with your approach and the tone of your brand.

Customization Phase:

- Customize the chosen template to suit your company and the specific guest blogging opportunity you are targeting. Ensure your email is personalized, concise, and clearly outlines the value you can bring to the host blog.

Writing Phase:

- In the space provided, write down your customized guest post outreach email for a specific guest post opportunity. Focus on making a strong introduction, proposing your guest post idea, and why it would be beneficial for their audience.

_____

_____

_____

_____

_____

_____

_____

_____

_____

_____

_____

_____

_____

10.1 | Weaving Your Story

Collect Stories:

- Reflect on your product/service journey, noting key milestones, customer feedback, and team experiences.
- Consult with sales and support teams for additional stories.

Record Stories:

- List 10 stories, including their sources and potential marketing uses.

Plan Usage:

- Identify how and where each story could be effectively utilized across your digital channels.

	Story	Source	Marketing Use
1.			
2.			
3.			
4.			
5.			
6.			
7.			
8.			
9.			
10.			

10.2 | Evoke, Engage, Email

1. Create your "Welcome Aboard" email with these steps.
2. Identify and articulate your business's core values and mission.
3. Write a short narrative showcasing these values in action.
4. Share a customer success story, highlighting how your business solved their problem.
5. End with a call-to-action that encourages reader engagement.

Define and list your business's core values and mission statement.
Craft a narrative that brings your brand's values to life.
Detail a real or hypothetical customer success story related to your brand. (refer to 10.1)
Develop a compelling call-to-action to conclude your email.

10.3 | Create (or Revise) Your Welcome Email Sequence

Outline Each Email:

- Detail the key components and objectives for each email in the sequence, incorporating storytelling where appropriate.

Refer to Your Story Bank:

- Revisit the stories listed in your story bank from exercise 10.1. Select relevant stories to weave into your educational emails to enhance engagement and relatability.

Email Step	Key Components & Objectives	Story Element to Include
Welcome Aboard	- Greet and introduce your brand. - Outline what subscribers can expect in terms of content and frequency. - Encourage open dialogue.	
Educational Email #1	- Introduce a fundamental concept related to your product/service.	
Educational Email #2	- Dive deeper into a specific aspect of your offering or industry.	
Educational Email #3	- Share advanced tips or strategies for getting the most out of your product/service.	
Special Offer Email	- Present a compelling offer or discount.	

10.4 | Nurture with Knowledge

Develop a three to five email lead magnet nurture sequence as follows:

1. Choose a lead magnet and related topic relevant to your audience's needs and interests.
2. Outline three to five key points or lessons to cover in the series.
3. Draft an outline for each email, focusing on how each part will introduce, discuss, and provide solutions.
4. Plan the schedule for sending out the series to ensure consistent engagement.

The lead magnet you will create a nurture sequence for:

Title	Short Description of Content	Send Out After " X " Days

11.1 | How Instagrammable Is Your Customer Experience?

1. Map out your customer journey from initial awareness to post-purchase experience.

2. For each stage of the journey, identify potential touchpoints where customers might be inclined to create and share content about their experience with your brand.

3. Brainstorm ideas for enhancing these touchpoints to encourage UGC creation and sharing.

Journey Stage	Touchpoint	Enhancement Ideas
Awareness		
Consideration		
Purchase		
Post-purchase		

Which touchpoints in your customer journey have the most potential for encouraging UGC?

_____

_____

_____

How can you align your UGC strategy with your brand's overall aesthetic and values?

_____

_____

_____

What resources or partnerships might you need to implement your ideas for enhancing the customer experience to increase organic creation of UGC?

_____

_____

_____

11.2 | Hashtag Hero

Step 1: Brainstorm Hashtag Ideas: Think about your brand values, products, and the message you want to convey. Come up with 5 potential hashtags that are branded, SEO-optimized, catchy, unique, and easy to remember. Remember, the purpose of this hashtag is to encourage the organic creation of UGC, so try to choose a hashtag that a customer who is a social media user might actually share.

1. _____
2. _____
3. _____
4. _____
5. _____

Step 2: Market Research: Research existing hashtags in your industry. Ensure your chosen hashtag is not already widely used, is different enough, and potentially resonates with your target audience.

Potential Hashtag	Existing Similar Hashtags	Target Audience

Step 3: Hashtag Launch Plan: Develop a launch plan for your hashtag. This should include initial posts from your brand introducing the hashtag, incentives for customers to use it (e.g., contests, features on your social media), and a schedule for regular engagement.

Launch Element	Description	Timeline
Initial Post		
Incentives		
Engagement Schedule		

Step 4: Engage and Amplify: Once your hashtag is live, regularly engage with posts that use it. Share the best content on your brand's channels and consider rewarding the most creative or impactful posts.

Content Type	Engagement Strategy	Amplification Plan
User Posts		
Brand Posts		

Step 5: Track and Adjust: Use social media analytics tools to track the reach and engagement of your hashtag. Be prepared to adjust your strategy based on what content performs best.

11.3 | Content Creator Collab Fest

Step 1: Content Creation Brief: Create a clear content brief that you will provide the content creator or UGC creator once you begin to collaborate. This should include the campaign goals, specific product focuses, brand guidelines, and any other relevant information to ensure the content aligns with your brand's objectives.

Campaign Goals	Product Focus	Brand Guidelines	Timeline

Step2: Identify Content Creators: Research and identify content creators within your niche who produce high-quality, engaging content that aligns with your brand's aesthetic and values. If you can't find suitable content creators, explore UGC creators on social media platforms by doing a search for #ugccreator or freelance marketplaces like Fiverr or Upwork.

Creator Name	Platform/Marketplace	Content Style & Quality (What you like about their content)

Step 3: Outreach and Negotiation: Reach out to the identified content creators or UGC creators with a personalized message expressing your interest in their work and proposing a potential collaboration. Discuss the scope of the project, including the type of content needed, timeline, and compensation (product or content creation fee).

Creator	Outreach Message Highlights	Collaboration Scope	Compensation

11.4 | Review Rally

Step 1: Customer Engagement & Incentivization: Identify customers or clients who have had a positive experience with your brand. Reach out to them personally, thanking them for their business and asking for a review. Consider offering incentives for leaving a review, such as discounts on future purchases, entry into a giveaway, or access to something exclusive.

Customer Name	Purchase Date	Outreach Method	Incentive Offered	Review Status

Step 2: Highlight, Share & Respond: Regularly highlight positive reviews and testimonials on your social media channels, website, and marketing materials. This not only showcases customer satisfaction but also encourages others to share their experiences.

Review/Testimonial	Source	Highlight Date	Sharing Channels	Response

Step 3: Analyze Trends: Use feedback from reviews to identify trends in customer satisfaction or areas for improvement. Implement changes based on this feedback to enhance the customer experience.

Trend Identified	Related Reviews	Improvement Actions	Implementation Date

PART FOUR – ALLOW GROWTH

Chapter Twelve – GROW CONTENT

Summary of Main Points:

1. **Content as a Long-Term Asset:** Content can be continually updated, repurposed, and refreshed across platforms to maximize its value over time while maintaining relevance and SEO performance.

2. **Strategic Content Creation:** Planning for repurposing from the start involves using versatile formats like video podcasts and livestreams that can be easily adapted for different platforms.

3. **Platform-Specific Content Adaptation:** To achieve the best results, content should be tailored to each social media platform's unique characteristics and user behaviors rather than simply reposted across all channels.

4. **Versatile Content Repurposing:** Both text-based and video content offer numerous repurposing opportunities, from transforming blog posts into various formats to breaking down longer videos into shorter, platform-appropriate segments.

Chapter Thirteen – GROW CONVERSATIONS

Summary of Main Points:

1. **Email Marketing Automation:** Allows for personalized, automated communication paths that can increase engagement and business growth while requiring the same effort from the business side.

2. **Transactional vs. Triggered Emails:** Differentiates between emails sent in response to a customer's direct action (transactional) and those designed to guide the customer journey based on their interactions (triggered).

3. **The Power of Transactional Emails:** These emails, due to their personalized and timely nature, have a significantly higher engagement and conversion rate compared to general promotional emails.

4. **Leveraging Transactional Emails for Business Growth:** Businesses can use transactional emails creatively to enhance customer engagement, upsell, and ultimately increase revenue.

5. **Emails in Customer Lifecycle and Retention:** Automated emails have a role in different stages of the customer lifecycle, from acquisition and engagement to re-engagement, and their impact on customer retention and revenue.

Chapter Fourteen – GROW INFLUENCE

Summary of Main Points:

1. **Definition and Evolution of Brand Ambassadors:** There has been a transition from traditional celebrity endorsements to current brand ambassadors who are social media users that genuinely love and promote the brand authentically.

2. **Types of Brand Ambassadors:** There are different types of ambassadors such as customers, employees, affiliate ambassadors, and expert ambassadors, each bringing unique value and engagement strategies to the brand.

3. **Creating a Brand Ambassador Program:** A step-by-step guide on how to set up a brand ambassador program, including identifying potential ambassadors, defining the program's goals, and the tools needed for management.

4. **Impact and Value of Brand Ambassadors:** The tangible benefits of having brand ambassadors include increased brand authenticity, wider reach, and deeper customer engagement that translates into higher conversion rates.

12.1 | Blog to Textual Threads

1. Select a blog post from your library of content that you want to repurpose into social media threads.
2. Identify the 5 to 10 main points of the blog post that you want to highlight in your threads.
3. Craft a captivating thread introduction that fits Twitter (maximum 280 chars.) and Threads (maximum 500 chars.) Remember, the last post in the thread should have a call-to-action with a link to the original blog post.
4. Summarize main points in concise, tweetable messages (280 chars/post) to create a cohesive Twitter thread.
5. Expand Twitter thread for Threads (500 chars/post), adding insights, examples, and tips for extra value.
6. Consider using a free tool like wordcounter.net to calculate character count in real-time.

Blog Post Title: _____   Blog Post URL: _____

Main Points:	1		6	
	2		7	
	3		8	
	4		9	
	5		10	
Introductory Twitter Thread (limit of 280 characters)				
	What can you end with to keep people reading the next thread?			
Introductory Threads Thread (limit of 500 characters)				
	What can you end with to keep people reading the next thread?			

12.2 | Blog to Image Carousel

1. Select a blog post to repurpose into image carousels.
2. Identify 5 main points to highlight.
3. Use a visual content tool (e.g., Adobe Express) to choose brand-aligned templates.
4. Create an eye-catching intro image optimized for Instagram and LinkedIn.
5. Visually represent each main point with a text summary to entice viewers to scroll to the next image.
6. Include a CTA on the last image directing readers to the original blog post.
7. Save carousels in square image format for Instagram and square PDF for LinkedIn.
8. Ensure carousels are visually cohesive, informative, and brand aligned.

Blog Post Title: _____ Blog Post URL: _____

Main Points:

1. _____

2. _____

3. _____

4. _____

5. _____

	Instagram Layout/Sketch/Description	LinkedIn Layout/Sketch/Description
Intro Image		
Main Point 1		
Main Point 2		
Main Point 3		
Main Point 4		
Main Point 5		
CTA Image		

12.3 | Blog to Video (Horizontal)

1. Choose a blog post to repurpose into a video.
2. Identify the 3 to 5 main points to cover in your video.
3. Decide on your preferred method: a. Write a script summarizing the main points, or b. Use the work from previous activities 12.1 and 12.2 to create bullet points (if repurposing the same blog post).
4. Set up your smartphone to record the video: a. Find a well-lit, quiet space. b. Use a tripod or stable surface to avoid shaky footage. c. Ensure your background is clean.
5. Record your video, following your script or bullet points. Aim for 3 to 5 minutes.
6. Optional - Edit your video using iMovie, CapCut, or Descript:
    a. Remove any awkward silences or filler words.
    b. Add transitions, text overlays, or other visual elements as desired.
7. Review your video for clarity, engagement, and alignment with your brand.
8. Consider if the video is optimized for Facebook, LinkedIn, or YouTube:
    a. Determine if any platform-specific changes are needed.
    b. Make necessary edits or create separate versions for each platform.
9. Upload your video to the chosen platforms and monitor its performance.

Blog Post Title: _____ Blog Post URL: _____

Main Points:

1	
2	
3	
4	
5	

Script or Bullet Points:

_____

_____

_____

_____

_____

_____

_____

_____

12.4 | Blog to Short-Form Video (Vertical)

1. Upload the horizontal video created in the previous activity to YouTube.
2. From your smartphone, navigate to your YouTube channel and find the uploaded video.
3. Locate the "Remix" button under the video and select it.
4. Choose the option to edit the video into a short.
5. Ensure the top right corner displays "15" for a 15-second video.
6. Using the bottom slider, select the most engaging or important 15-second segment.
7. Click "Done" to confirm your selection.
8. Add relevant text and a filter to enhance the video's visual appeal.
9. Press "Next" to proceed.
10. Choose an eye-catching thumbnail for your short by clicking on the best still frame from your video.
11. Create a compelling caption to accompany your short-form video.
12. While uploading is optional for this exercise, recognize the potential for repurposing video assets.
13. Explore tools recommended in the Tools Glossary to streamline the video creation process.

Horizontal Video Title: _____ YouTube URL: _____

Main Point for Short-Form Video: _____

Timestamp: Start: _____ End: _____

Text Overlay: _____ Filter: _____

Thumbnail: _____ Caption: _____

Short-Form Video Details: Platform: □ YouTube Shorts   □ Instagram Reels   □ TikTok

□ Facebook Reels   □ LinkedIn   □ X (formerly Twitter)   □ Pinterest

	AI Tool Exploration (see Tools Glossary)
Tool 1:	
Notes:	
Tool 2:	
Notes:	
Tool 3:	
Notes:	

Insights: _____

Next Steps: _____

12.5 | Reflections on Content Repurposing

1. Review the content repurposing activities you completed in this chapter.
2. Reflect on how these activities have influenced your perspective on content creation.
3. Identify ways to create content with repurposing in mind from the outset.
4. Assess whether creating video content was easier than anticipated.
5. List the specific challenges you encountered during the repurposing process.
6. Refer to the Tools Glossary at the end of this workbook to identify solutions for your challenges.
7. Develop a plan to integrate content repurposing into your overall content strategy.
8. Set achievable goals for implementing your repurposing plan and track your progress.

Insights Gained: _____

_____

_____

_____

Creating Content through Repurposing Thoughts: _____

_____

_____

Video Creation Experience: ☐ Easier than expected   ☐ As expected   ☐ More challenging

Results: (Views & Engagement) ☐ More than expected   ☐ As expected   ☐ Less than Expected

AI Tools to Explore (see Tools Glossary)			
Tool 1:		Purpose:	
Tool 2:		Purpose:	
Tool 3:		Purpose:	
Tool 4:		Purpose:	
Tool 5:		Purpose:	

Reflections and Next Steps: _____

_____

13.1 | Don't Abandon Me

1. Identify the key reasons why customers might abandon their shopping cart in your business.
2. Determine the content for each of the three emails in your sequence: a. Email 1: Reminder and support b. Email 2: Incentive or social proof c. Email 3: Urgency and final offer
3. Decide on the timing between each email (e.g., 2 hours, 24 hours, 48 hours).
4. Write compelling subject lines and email copy for each email in the cart abandonment sequence.
5. Include clear calls-to-action (CTAs) in each email to encourage customers to complete their purchase.
6. Review and refine your email sequence for clarity, persuasiveness, and brand consistency.

Key Reasons for Cart Abandonment

_____

_____

Reminder and Support

Email 1	Sent after how many hours?	Message:
	Call to Action (CTA)	

Incentive or Social Proof

Email 2	Sent after how many hours?	Message:
	Call to Action (CTA)	

Urgency and Final Offer

Email 3	Sent after how many hours?	Message:
	Call to Action (CTA)	

Results:

_____

13.2 | It Doesn't Have to Be a Transaction

1. Choose a transactional email type (e.g., Order Confirmation, Account Activation, Shipping Confirmation, or How Was Everything?) or create your own.
2. Identify the key information to include in the email (e.g., order details, tracking information, support resources).
3. Determine how you can use this email to build trust and develop a relationship with your customer (e.g., personalized recommendations, helpful tips, or a sincere thank you) above and beyond the key information.
4. Write a compelling subject line and email copy that incorporates both the transactional information and the relationship-building content.
5. Include a clear call-to-action (CTA) that encourages customers to engage further with your brand.
6. Review and refine your email for clarity, tone, and brand consistency.

Transactional Type Email: _____

Key Information Included:

_____

_____

_____

Relationship Building Content:

_____

_____

_____

Email Draft:

Subject:	
Content:	
CTA:	

Reflection:

13.3 │ Score Your List

Note: Confirm what sort of social scoring your current email marketing software provider has. The following exercise is based on your ability to create a scoring system in your software on a contact-by-contact basis. Your software might only provide a 5-star rating of your contacts that is automated. In that case, think about how you can segment your list based on the 5 stars and think of different things that you can send 3-star (low score), 4-star (mid score), and 5-star (high score) contacts.

1. List the key actions that demonstrate a contact's interest in your business (e.g., website visits, email opens, clicks, downloads).
2. Assign a point value, from 1 to 10, to each action based on its importance and relevance to your business.
3. Determine the expiration time for each action (e.g., 30 days, 60 days, 90 days).
4. Create a scoring table that outlines the actions, point values, and expiration times.
5. Brainstorm ideas for triggered emails based on different score thresholds (e.g., high-score welcome series, mid-score re-engagement campaign, low-score winback offer).
6. Reflect on how this scoring system can help you better understand and segment your email list for more effective marketing.

	Action	Point Value	Expiration Time
1			
2			
3			
4			
5			

Triggered Email Ideas

	Points	Ideas
Low Score		
Mid Score		
High Score		

Reflection:

13.4 | Re-Engage!

1. Determine the inactive period after which you will send re-engagement emails (e.g., 90/180 days).
2. Plan the content for your re-engagement email(s), focusing on: a. Reminding subscribers of your brand's value b. Incentivizing them to re-engage (e.g., special offer, exclusive content) c. Asking for feedback or preferences
3. Decide on the number of emails in your re-engagement series (e.g., 1, 2, or 3 emails) and the time interval between each email.
4. Write compelling subject lines and email copy for each email in the series, incorporating the planned content and clear calls-to-action (CTAs).
5. Determine the criteria for removing non-responsive subscribers from your list after the re-engagement campaign.
6. Review and refine your re-engagement campaign for clarity, persuasiveness, and brand consistency.

Inactive Period	(circle one)	90 days	120 days	180 days	other:
	Sent after How Many Days	Subject	Content		CTA
Email 1					
Email 2					
Email 3					

Removal Criteria:

_____

_____

_____

65

14.1 | Defining Your Brand Ambassadors

1. List 5 potential brand ambassadors for each category (Customer, Employee, Affiliate, and Expert.)
2. For each potential ambassador, describe why you think they would be a good fit or what parameters you used to choose them.

	Potential Ambassador	Reason for Selection
Customer		
Employee		
Affiliate		
Expert		

14.2 | The Recruitment Game

1. For each category of Brand Ambassador (Customer, Employee, Affiliate, and Expert), brainstorm 3-5 recruitment strategies or efforts.
2. Consider the unique characteristics and motivations of each ambassador type when developing your strategies.

	Recruitment Strategy
Customer Ambassador	
Employee Ambassador	
Affiliate Ambassador	
Expert Ambassador	

14.3 | The Give and Take

1. For each ambassador type (Customer, Employee, Affiliate, and Expert), list 3-5 potential "asks" or activities you would like them to perform.
2. For each ambassador type, brainstorm 3-5 incentives or benefits you can offer to encourage participation and loyalty.

	Asks/Activities	Incentives/Benefits
Customer Ambassador		
Employee Ambassador		
Affiliate Ambassador		
Expert Ambassador		

14.4 | Fleshing Out the Complete Strategy

1. Define clear goals for your Brand Ambassador program, including strategy and KPIs.
2. Outline a structured communication plan between your company and all Brand Ambassadors.
3. List potential training and resources you can provide to support your Brand Ambassadors.
4. Brainstorm content creation support you can offer to help Brand Ambassadors create engaging content.
5. Develop ideas for recognition, awards, travel, or other ways to acknowledge high-performing Brand Ambassadors and make them role models.

Program Goals and KPIs:

Communication Plan:

Training & Resources:

Content Creation Support:

Recognition & Awards:

PART FIVE – SCALE

Chapter Fifteen – SCALE INFLUENCE

Summary of Main Points:

1. **Diverse Spectrum of Influencers:** While influencers have been traditionally categorized in terms of follower size from nano to mega, focus on engagement quality over follower count.

2. **Authentic Collaboration:** Focus on developing genuine partnerships and remember that effective influencer marketing relies on mutual benefit rather than control.

3. **Building Brand Influence:** Brands should enhance their own influence to naturally attract external influencers and generate inbound interest from content creators.

4. **Engagement Strategies:** There are various methods for collaborating with influencers, including product gifting, paid collaborations, and affiliate marketing.

5. **Beyond Social Media:** The scope of influencer marketing is wide, and you should look to expand influencer collaborations to include SEO, podcast advertising, and even email newsletters.

Chapter Sixteen – SCALE BUDGET

Summary of Main Points:

1. **Strategic Foundation First:** Prioritize optimizing organic digital marketing channels before allocating budgets to paid media to ensure funds enhance already successful efforts.

2. **Bridging Visibility Gaps:** Use paid media to improve visibility where organic reach is limited, ensuring content reaches the target audience across multiple platforms.

3. **Retargeting for Engagement:** Emphasize retargeting to connect with users who have previously interacted with the brand, capitalizing on their higher potential for conversion.

4. **Time-Sensitive Campaigns:** Employ paid media for promoting urgent messages, such as events or sales, to quickly attract attention despite the audience's familiarity with the brand.

5. **Targeting and Objectives:** Focus on detailed targeting options and clear campaign objectives to reach the most relevant audience and achieve specific marketing goals effectively.

Chapter Seventeen – PDCA

Summary of Main Points:

1. **The Importance of Measurable Outcomes:** Set quantifiable goals to efficiently gauge and enhance marketing efforts.

2. **Continuous Improvement Through PDCA:** Apply the PDCA cycle to refine digital marketing strategies continuously, ensuring adaptive practices.

3. **Data-Driven Decision Making:** Leverage data for informed decision-making, aiding in optimizing marketing channels for better ROI.

4. **The Value of Experimentation:** Always have an experimental mindset, using PDCA to test various marketing tactics.

5. **Strategic Approach to Budgeting:** How PDCA guides strategic budget allocation, focusing resources on high-impact activities.

Chapter Eighteen – SCALE PEOPLE

Summary of Main Points:

1. **Outsourcing as a Growth Strategy:** Utilize freelance marketplaces like Fiverr and Upwork to access skilled professionals worldwide, emphasizing the need to delegate tasks to focus on core business activities.

2. **Skill Specialization and Flexibility:** Consider hiring freelancers with specialized skills for specific tasks, providing flexibility and efficiency in operations.

3. **Cost Efficiency:** Outsourcing can have cost advantages over traditional employment, including lower overhead costs and the ability to scale up or down easily.

4. **Experimentation and Scaling:** Consider hiring multiple freelancers for test projects to identify the best fit and how you can scale business operations through strategic outsourcing.

Chapter Nineteen – AI & MARKETING

Summary of Main Points:

1. **Generative AI Revolution**: Generative AI is impacting businesses large and small, helping you create diverse types of content types and transforming marketing strategies with efficiency and innovation.

2. **Media Applications**: Generative AI can be leveraged to help create and improve a wide variety of content mediums, including text, image, video, and audio content.

3. **Workflow Integration**: AI tools can be seamlessly incorporated into marketing processes, enhancing content planning, production, and optimization.

4. **Success Stories**: Businesses are already leveraging AI for significant marketing improvements.

5. **Ethical Considerations**: It is important to address potential ethical issues in AI use and therefore consider establishing policies that ensure responsible use of AI.

Chapter Twenty – SCALE TECHNOLOGY

Summary of Main Points:

1. **Strategic Use of Technology in Marketing**: Leverage technology not just for its own sake but as a strategic component to enhance and scale digital marketing efforts effectively.

2. **Search Engine Optimization (SEO) and Content Creation**: There are a plethora of tools and techniques for improving search engine visibility and creating SEO-optimized content. It is important to adapt content to meet SEO standards through tools that offer insights on keyword research, content performance, and competitive analysis.

3. **Multimedia Content Optimization**: There are also a multitude of tools for video and audio content creation, editing, and optimization, including platforms that support high-quality recording, livestreaming, and podcast hosting, to enhance content engagement across various media formats.

4. **Email Marketing and Automation**: Tools can also aid in creating, distributing, and integrating lead magnets with email marketing efforts, along with marketing automation software that enhances customer engagement and lead nurturing processes.

5. **Social Media Engagement and Paid Advertising**: Companies should strategically select and use social media marketing tools to maintain authentic engagement and utilize AI for generating effective ad copy and creatives. It is critical to maintain a balance between automation and human touch.

15.1 | How Will You Collab with External Influencers?

1. Choose a collaboration type (e.g., gifting product, paid collab for sponsored content, affiliate marketing) or develop your own idea based on your experience.
2. Determine the specific activity you will collaborate on with the influencer.
3. List the "give" or the things you can potentially provide the influencer as part of the collaboration.
4. Outline the "take" or specific things you would like the influencer to do for you in return.
5. Review your plan to ensure it aligns with your brand's goals and resources.

Collaboration Type: _____

Specific Activity: _____

_____

_____

Your Give	Your Take

Review & Reflection: _____

_____

_____

15.2 | Mapping Your Influence Ecosystem

1. Choose your most strategic social network and keyword that describes your product or service.
2. Conduct a search in the social network using the keyword or relevant hashtag and analyze the content that appears in the search results.
3. Identify 10 content creators from the search results whose content you think would attract your target audience.
4. For each potential influencer, record the following information:
   1. Social network username
   2. Number of followers
   3. Average engagement for the last 5 posts
   4. Average engagement ratio (average engagement / number of followers)
   5. Qualitative aspects you liked about their content
   6. Why you think they are a good fit to promote your brand
5. Review your list of potential influencers and prioritize them based on their alignment with your brand and engagement metrics.

Social Network: _____   Keyword/Hashtag: _____

Priority Order	Username	Followers	Avg. Engagement	Engagement Ratio	Content Quality	Brand Fit

15.3 | Crafting Your Influencer Outreach Campaign

1. Review your list of 10 potential influencers from Activity 15.2 and select 5 to engage with based on your priority order.
2. For each of the 5 influencers, create a short, personalized outreach message that includes:
   - Why you want to collaborate with them
   - How you would like to collaborate (based on your ideas from Activity 15.1)
   - What's in it for them (WIIFM) - the benefits and incentives for the influencer
3. Ensure each message is tailored to the individual influencer and showcases your genuine interest in their content and brand.
4. Review and refine your outreach messages for clarity, persuasiveness, and alignment with your brand's voice and goals.

Influencer 1 (Name – Username)	@
Outreach Message:	

Influencer 2 (Name – Username)	@
Outreach Message:	

Influencer 3 (Name – Username)	@
Outreach Message:	

Influencer 4 (Name – Username)	@
Outreach Message:	

Influencer 5 (Name – Username)	@
Outreach Message:	

16.1 | The Spending Efficiency Audit

1. List all current digital marketing channels where you are investing (e.g., social media ads, search engine marketing, and other paid media efforts).
2. For each channel, document the following metrics over the last month, quarter, year-to-date or previous year:
   - Expenses
   - Reach
   - Engagement
   - Conversion
   - Return on Investment (ROI)
3. Compare performance metrics to identify underperforming channels.
4. Brainstorm alternative strategies for reallocating budgets from underperforming channels to those with higher ROI or growth potential.
5. Develop a plan to test new budget allocations over the next time period, setting specific Key Performance Indicators (KPIs) to measure success.

Time Period Selected:

Channel	Expenses	Reach	Engagement	Conversions (Number/Amount)	ROI

Underperforming Channels:	Reallocation Strategies

Testing Plan:	KPIs:

16.2 | Targeting Mastery Workshop

1. Identify three different target audiences for your product or service based on:
   - Demographics
   - Interests
   - Behaviors
2. For each target audience, develop a hypothetical paid media campaign specifying:
   - Platform
   - Targeting options (e.g., interest-based, custom audiences, lookalike audiences)
   - Ad type (e.g., video, carousel)
3. Outline the campaign's objective (awareness, consideration, conversion) and how the chosen targeting options align with this objective.

Target Audience Used		Ad Creative Idea	
Platform	Targeting Options	Ad Type	
Campaign Objective		Alignment Rationale	

Target Audience Used		Ad Creative Idea	
Platform	Targeting Options	Ad Type	
Campaign Objective		Alignment Rationale	

Target Audience Used		Ad Creative Idea	
Platform	Targeting Options	Ad Type	
Campaign Objective		Alignment Rationale	

16.3 | Funnel Focus Group

1. Sketch out the marketing funnel for your business, identifying key characteristics and needs of potential customers at each stage.
2. Develop a specific paid media campaign for each stage of the funnel, selecting appropriate platforms and ad types based on the stage's objectives:
   - Awareness
   - Consideration
   - Conversion
3. Assign metrics to each campaign that will measure its success in moving targets to the next stage of the funnel.
4. Implement one of the campaigns on a small scale as a pilot test.
5. Analyze pilot test results, identify lessons learned, and plan adjustments for scaling the campaign.

Marketing Funnel Sketch:

	Platform	Ad Type	Metrics
Awareness Campaign			
Consideration Campaign			
Conversion Campaign			

	Campaign Chosen:	Implementation Plan:
Pilot Test Details:		
Pilot Test Results & Analysis:		
Scaling Adjustments:		

16.4 | The ROI Revolution

1. Select two to three recent digital marketing campaigns you have run.
2. Gather relevant data for each campaign, including:
   - Cost
   - Reach
   - Engagements
   - Conversions
   - Other metrics impacting ROI
3. Calculate the ROI for each campaign, analyzing factors contributing to success or underperformance.
4. Based on your analysis, identify patterns or insights that could inform future campaign strategies.
5. Create a plan to adjust future marketing efforts based on ROI findings, focusing on enhancing high-performing strategies and addressing areas of weakness.

Metrics	Campaign 1 Name:	Campaign 2 Name:	Campaign 3 Name:
Cost			
Reach			
Engagements			
Conversions (Number/Amount)			
Other			
ROI			
Success Factors			
Underperformance Factors			

Pattern Insights	
Adjustment Plan	

17.1 | The PDCA Cycle in Action: A Social Media Experiment

- **Plan:**
  1. Choose a specific social media platform and a marketing objective (e.g., increase engagement, drive website traffic).
  2. Develop a hypothesis for a strategy or tactic that you believe will help achieve the objective.
  3. Set a timeframe for the experiment (I recommend at least 1 month) and define the metrics you will track to measure success.
- **Do:**
  1. Implement the strategy or tactic as planned.
  2. Consistently execute the plan throughout the defined timeframe.
- **Check:**
  1. At the end of the experiment, gather and analyze the data related to your defined metrics.
  2. Compare the results to your initial hypothesis and past performance.
- **Act:**
  1. Based on the analysis, determine if the experiment was a success or if adjustments are needed.
  2. If successful, consider how to integrate the strategy or tactic into your ongoing social media efforts.
  3. If unsuccessful, use the learnings to develop a new hypothesis and plan for your next experiment.
- Repeat the PDCA cycle with a new experiment, continuously improving your social media marketing efforts.

Plan	**Social Media Platform:**	
	Marketing Objective:	
	Hypothesis:	
	Timeframe:	
	Metrics to Track:	
Do	**Implementation Notes:**	
Check	**Results:**	
	Comparison to Hypothesis:	
	Comparison to Past Performance:	
Act	**Experiment Success:**	☐ Yes ☐ No
	Integration Plan (if successful):	
	New Hypothesis (if unsuccessful);	
	Next Experiment:	

17.2 | Create PDCA KPIs

1. Review the top, middle, and bottom of the funnel metrics discussed in the chapter.
2. Identify the metrics that are most relevant to your business and marketing objectives.
3. For each selected metric, gather historical data from your digital marketing efforts.
4. Calculate the average performance for each metric over a specific timeframe (e.g., last "X" months).
5. Set these averages as your baseline KPIs for future experiments and marketing efforts.
6. Compare your baseline KPIs to how you did in the previous time period.
7. Continuously update and refine your KPIs as you gather more data and insights.

Top of Funnel KPIs		
Metric	**Baseline**	**Previous Time Period Performance**

Middle of Funnel KPIs		
Metric	**Baseline**	**Previous Time Period Performance**

Bottom of Funnel KPIs		
Metric	**Baseline**	**Previous Time Period Performance**

Reflections on Comparisons & Next Steps:

_____

_____

_____

17.3 | Create Your Digital Threads Report

1. Using the KPIs identified in Activity 17.2, create a spreadsheet or document template for your monthly report.
2. For each KPI, include the following columns:
   - Metric Name
   - Baseline KPI
   - Budget/Target
   - Actual Performance
   - Variance (Actual vs. Budget)
   - Insights/Notes
3. Set up formulas or calculations to automatically determine the variance between actual performance and budget/target.
4. Include a section for overall insights, learnings, and action items based on the monthly performance.
5. Use this template to create your monthly Digital Threads report, filling in the actual performance data and updating the budget/target as needed.
6. Continuously refine and improve your report template as you gather more data and insights.

Monthly Digital Threads Report Template:

Metric Name	Baseline KPI	Budget/Target	Actual Performance	Variance	Insights/Notes
Overall Insights & Action Items					
Next Steps:					

18.1 | What Should I Outsource

1. Review your current digital marketing efforts and identify areas where you lack expertise, time, or resources.
2. From this list, choose one specific task that you believe would have the most significant impact if outsourced successfully.
3. Write a detailed description of the task, including its purpose, scope, and any specific requirements or constraints.
4. Define the skills, experience, and qualities you would look for in an ideal candidate to handle this task.
5. Establish clear, measurable success criteria for the outsourced work, focusing on outcomes that align with your overall digital marketing goals.

Task to Outsource: _____

Task Description: _____

_____

_____

_____

Ideal Candidate Requirements: _____

_____

_____

_____

Success Criteria: _____

_____

_____

_____

Reflection: _____

_____

_____

18.2 | Crafting a Compelling Project Brief

1. Based on the previous work you did in Exercise 18.1, begin with a concise summary of the project, highlighting its purpose and key objectives.
2. Detail the scope of work, including specific deliverables, milestones, and deadlines.
3. Provide relevant background information about your business, target audience, and any specific context that will help the freelancer understand the project better.
4. Clearly outline your expectations for communication, progress updates, and any necessary approvals or feedback loops.
5. Include any relevant brand guidelines, reference materials, or examples that will help guide the freelancer's work.
6. Specify your budget or pricing expectations, and any other project constraints or requirements.
7. Consider targeted interview questions that will help you evaluate them (specific experience, availability, pricing guidelines, etc.)
8. Close with a call to action, inviting the freelancer to ask questions or provide their proposal for the work.

Project Summary:
Scope of Work:
• Deliverables:
• Milestones:
• Deadlines:
Background Information:
Communication Expectations:
Brand Guidelines & Reference Materials:
Budget & Pricing:
Interview Questions:
Call to Action:

18.3 | Find Your Freelancer

1. Using the task description and ideal candidate requirements from Activity 18.1, search for relevant freelancers or agencies on at least two freelance marketplaces (e.g., Fiverr, Upwork).
2. Utilize the platform's search and filter features to refine your results based on skills, experience, ratings, and pricing.
3. Select 3-5 potential candidates that best match your requirements and save their profiles for further evaluation.
4. Reach out to the selected candidates with your project brief, from Exercise 18.2, inquiring about their process, availability, and requesting a quote for the work.
5. Evaluate the responses based on their understanding of the project, proposed solutions, communication style, and value for money.

Freelance Marketplaces:	
1.	
2.	
Potential Candidates	
Name:	Platform:
Skills/Experience:	
Name:	Platform:
Skills/Experience:	
Name:	Platform:
Skills/Experience:	
Name:	Platform:
Skills/Experience:	
Name:	Platform:
Skills/Experience:	

18.4 | Evaluating Freelancer Proposals

1. Compile all the proposals received from freelancers for the outsourced task.
2. Create a list of evaluation criteria based on the project requirements, such as:
   - Understanding of the project scope and objectives
   - Relevance and quality of proposed solutions
   - Experience and expertise in the required skills
   - Communication and professionalism
   - Pricing and value for money
3. Assign weight to each criterion based on its importance to the project's success.
4. Review each proposal and score it against the defined criteria.
5. Calculate the total weighted score for each proposal and rank them accordingly.
6. Select the top 2-3 candidates based on their scores and conduct interviews or further discussions to make a final decision.

Evaluation Criteria	Weight

Evaluation Criteria						
Freelancer	Criterion 1	Criterion 2	Criterion 3	Criterion 4	Criterion 5	Total Score
1.						
2.						
3.						
4.						
5.						

Top Candidates:

Final Decision:

18.5 | Building Long-term Freelancer Relationships

1. Identify freelancers who have consistently delivered high-quality work and demonstrated a strong understanding of your business needs.
2. Schedule regular check-ins or progress updates to maintain open communication and address any issues or concerns proactively.
3. Provide constructive feedback on completed work, highlighting areas of excellence, and suggesting improvements where necessary.
4. Explore opportunities to offer additional projects or responsibilities to top-performing freelancers, fostering a sense of partnership and loyalty.
5. Implement a recognition or reward system for outstanding work, such as bonuses, referrals, or public acknowledgment.
6. Encourage freelancers to provide feedback on their experience working with your business and use this insight to continually improve your outsourcing processes.

Top-Performing Freelancers:		
Communication Plan:		
Feedback Process:		
Growth Opportunities:		
1.		
2.		
3.		
Recognition & Rewards:		
Continuous Improvement:		

19.1 | Let the AI Experiment Begin

1. Go to Google Gemini (https://gemini.google.com/app).
2. Copy and paste the following prompt into the text box, replacing the bracketed information with details specific to your business:
    1. "I am an online store that provides [type of products and services] to [general target audience]. Our most popular products include [describe your 1 to 3 top selling products]. My company's key differentiators are [list 2 differentiators]. Our target audience are [describe your target audience in more detail]. What are 10 blog post titles that you recommend we write to speak to the pain points of our target audience and build trust with them through our content?"
3. Press enter and review the generated blog post titles.
4. Reflect on the results:
    1. Are they helpful and on target?
    2. How could you use these ideas for Platform Authentic Content or newsletter content?
    3. What new ways of using AI for content creation did this exercise inspire?
5. Refine the prompt based on your reflections and run it again to see if the results improve.

Your Personalized Prompt:

I am an online store (or business) that provides _____ to _____. Our most popular products include _____. My company's key differentiators are _____. Our target audience are/is _____.

Generated Blog Post Titles	
1.	
2.	
3.	
4.	
5.	
6.	
7.	
8.	
9.	
10.	

Refined Prompt & Reflection: _____

_____

_____

19.2 │ Textual AI for Social Media

1. Choose one of your own blog posts or copy and paste one from my own website (https://nealschaffer.com/new-blog-posts/).
2. Go to Google Gemini (https://gemini.google.com/app).
3. Enter the following prompts in order: a. First Prompt: "For the following blog post I want you to create various content for social media. First, I will enter the blog post and then enter each prompt separately for the content I would like you to create. Are you ready?" b. Second Prompt: Paste the entire blog post.
4. Review the AI-generated content for social media.
5. Evaluate the content:
   - Is it usable as-is, or does it require editing?
   - What tweaks could you make to the prompt to improve the output?
6. Reflect on how this exercise has changed your perspective on using AI for content repurposing.

Blog Post Title:		Blog Post URL:	
AI-Generated Social Media Content:			
Evaluation: Usability: □ As-Is	□ Requires Editing	□ Start All Over	

Potential Prompt Tweaks: _____

_____

_____

Reflection: _____

_____

_____

19.3 | Visual AI for Marketing

1. Go to the free Adobe Firefly website (https://firefly.adobe.com/) and sign up if required.
2. Enter the following prompt or create your own based on your business: "a pair of florescent green soccer cleats next to a soccer ball on a beautifully lit soccer field at night with stadium lights shining brightly."
3. Review the AI-generated image.
4. Reflect on the potential applications: Imagine if you were a soccer cleat brand and could replace the cleats with your own. Could you use AI-generated images to replace your product photography?
5. How could you use AI-generated visuals on your website, newsletters, or blog posts?
6. Refine the prompt based on your reflections and run it again to see if the results improve.

Prompt:

_____

_____

AI Generated Image:

Applications:	
Product Photography	
Website	
Newsletter	
Blog Post	
Social Media Post	

Refined Prompt:

_____

_____

19.4 | The AI Workflow

1. Review the sample content creation workflow in Chapter 19.
2. Create your own workflow diagram, specifying who is responsible for each stage and what tools you currently use.
3. Research the AI functionality of your current tools and identify areas where AI could be integrated to improve efficiency or quality.
4. Update your workflow diagram to include AI tools and their specific applications.
5. Refer to the Tools Glossary in the back of this workbook to discover new AI tools that could further enhance your workflow.

Current Workflow:

AI Integration Opportunities:

Updated Workflow with AI:

New AI Tools to Explore:

20.1 | SEO Tool Audit

1. List your current SEO tool in the first column.
2. Research 3 alternative SEO tools using the Tools Glossary at the end of this workbook and list them in the subsequent columns.
3. Complete the table below for each tool.
4. In the last column, make notes on which tool you prefer or provide more details on specific features.
5. Based on your analysis, decide whether to stick with your current tool or switch to a new one.

Feature	Current Tool	Option 1	Option 2	Option 3	Notes
Monthly Price					
Keyword Research					
PPC Keyword Research					
Competitor Analysis					
Backlink Research					
Link Building Advice					
Keyword Rank Tracker					
On-Page SEO Advice					
Local SEO Features					
Website Audit					
AI Features					

Decision:

20.2 | Email Marketing Tool Audit

1. Estimate your number of email subscribers in 12 months. This will be the number you base monthly pricing off of (If the email marketing software charges by number of emails sent per month, multiply your number of subscribers by 4 for an estimate).
2. List your current email marketing tool in the first column.
3. Research 3 alternative email marketing tools using the Tools Glossary at the end of this workbook and list them in the subsequent columns.
4. Complete the table below for each tool.
5. In the last column, make notes on which tool you prefer or provide more details on specific features.
6. Based on your analysis, decide whether to stick with your current tool or switch to a new one.

Estimated Subscribers:

Feature	Current Tool	Option 1	Option 2	Option 3	Notes
Monthly Price					
Landing Pages					
Sign-up Forms					
Visual Automations					
A/B Testing					
CRM Functionality					
Lead Scoring					
Transactional Emails					
SMS Sending					
Integrations					
AI Features					

Decision:

20.3 | Social Media Dashboard Tool Audit

1. List your current social media dashboard in the first column.
2. Research 3 alternative social media dashboards using the Tools Glossary at the end of this workbook and list them in the subsequent columns.
3. Complete the table below for each tool.
4. In the last column, make notes on which tool you prefer or provide more details on specific features.
5. Based on your analysis, decide whether to stick with your current tool or switch to a new one.

Feature	Current Tool	Option 1	Option 2	Option 3	Notes
Monthly Price					
Supported Platforms					
Post Schedular					
Best Post Time Recommendations					
Visual Content Calendar					
Bulk Scheduling (CSV)					
RSS Feeds Import					
Automation Features					
Social Inbox					
Analytics					
Collaborations Features					
AI Features					

Decision:

Digital Threads Tools Glossary

This is a companion section to Chapter 20: Scale Technology in *Digital Threads*.

As the marketing technology landscape changes rapidly, it made little sense to add names of specific companies to *Digital Threads* when the technology—and my recommendations— might change soon. That is why the *Digital Threads Companion Workbook* includes this section, which was originally an integral part of that chapter, and I will be regularly updating it.

What follows is a breakdown of my shortlist of recommended tools to help you implement each of the Digital Threads. Please refer to Chapter 20 in *Digital Threads* to understand the functionality of each type of tool listed.

Over the years, even before running the now defunct Social Tools Summit, I have had LOTS of marketing technology companies reach out to me for my opinion on their tool. They often want to collaborate or want me to become an affiliate, etc. So, there is a disclaimer that for a lot of these tools, I have an affiliate relationship, but no one has paid me to mention their tool in this book.

SEO Dashboard

The tool that I am a religious user of is Ubersuggest, currently the most reasonably priced tool for small businesses, but there are other tools to choose from that have their strengths and weaknesses.

- Semrush
- Ahrefs
- Moz
- SE Ranking
- Ubersuggest

SEO-Optimized Content Creation Tools

These tools are relatively new, but for this type of tool, I use Frase, and I use it religiously for every piece of content I create or revise when I want to optimize it for SEO. There are other options that you should investigate as each of these tools uses AI and has a different view of SEO optimized content and scoring.

- Frase
- Surfer
- MarketMuse
- Scalenut
- INK

YouTube SEO

TubeBuddy and VidIQ are the definitive two tools for YouTube SEO that are very similar but offer different functionality, especially with AI. Many YouTubers I know, as well as yours truly, actually subscribe to both tools to get the best of both worlds. These two tools offer you a myriad of options to help you ideate, create, and ultimately optimize each video to rank higher on YouTube.

- TubeBuddy
- VidIQ

Video Livestreaming

Another important component of these tools is the ability to livestream that content to popular platforms such as YouTube, LinkedIn, Facebook, Twitter, Instagram, and TikTok. While not every platform will live stream everywhere, you will want to take advantage of this functionality to get the most juice out of your content. I currently use Streamyard for this purpose.

- Streamyard
- Riverside
- Restream
- Zoom
- OBS Studio

Video Creation and Editing

You have a plethora of choices here for video creation, ranging from recording yourself using your smartphone or the pre-installed software on your computer, to using a desktop solution like Camtasia (Windows and Mac) and ScreenFlow (Mac only), or even something as simple as Zoom or Loom. Davinci Resolve and Capcut represent the new generation of video editing apps, while Descript relies on AI technology to help you more rapidly and effectively edit your video.

- Camtasia
- ScreenFlow
- Davinci Resolve
- Capcut
- Descript

Audio Content

Regarding podcast hosting sites, I use Buzzsprout for my Your Digital Marketing Coach podcast, and it comes as highly recommended, especially for their innovative approach to integrating AI into their product.

- Buzzsprout
- Captivate
- Libsyn
- Blubrry
- Fusebox

Audio Editing

Editing an audio for a podcast is like editing a video for YouTube: You either have an internal resource to help you do it or you end up outsourcing the task, which is what I do. However, should you wish to edit yourself, I recommend these tools:

- Descript
- Adobe Audition
- Audacity
- Auphonic
- Garage Band

Content Repurposing

Any of the above video livestreaming tools will provide you with raw video and audio files. These you can easily repurpose for blog posts, social media posts, ebooks and lead magnets, email newsletters, or short form video for social media.

For any text purposes, you will first need to use a tool to transcribe the audio file as accurately as possible. AI tools are getting better at this, and I am currently using Castmagic for this purpose. Other AI audio to text tools I would currently recommend include:

- Otter.ai
- Descript
- Castmagic
- Sonix
- Trint

There is no one killer app that will do all this repurposing for us across blog posts, social media posts, and longer content, so I would recommend a combination of the following two types of apps, both infused with AI features.

The first would be what are now referred to as AI podcast content generator tools, which also generate transcripts. Even if you do not plan on running a podcast, you can still use these tools to upload your audio and take advantage of the assets that they will automagically repurpose for you. Here is my shortlist, including the two tools I currently use:

- Buzzsprout Cohost (currently using)
- Castmagic (currently using)
- Podsqueeze
- Podium

The other option for converting your podcast transcript into a marketing asset is simply to use an AI content tool, free or paid, and prompt it to "create a xx-word social media post for xx network" or "create a xx-word summary of this for my email newsletter" etc. For social media specifically, you could use a social media dashboard like SocialBee that already has this functionality embedded, but if you were looking for a dedicated AI content tool, try:

- Jasper
- Tailwind Ghostwriter
- Copy.ai
- Writesonic
- Rytr

There are AI-powered software tools that can help you both find and repurpose your content to make short vertical videos that you can edit and then upload to the social media platform of your choice. This is one type of AI tool that is absolutely exploding in terms of the number of companies offering this technology, including:

- Opus Clip
- Pictory
- Vidyo
- Munch
- Wisecut

EMAIL TOOLS

Lead Magnet Creation Tools

If you want to create a textual lead magnet or something more interactive, a shortlist of the tools that can help you create or provide you with a customizable lead magnet to integrate into your website would be:

- Canva—If you are looking to create an ebook, searching for "ebook lead magnet" on Canva reveals literally thousands of ebook templates that you can use. You can also purchase attractive Canva ebook templates on Etsy for a very cheap price if you can't find what you are looking for directly on Canva.

- Visme—Another popular graphic design tool that can help you easily create a lead magnet through its nearly two dozen templates, including those for ebooks, checklists, worksheets, workbooks, cheat sheets, planners, and more.

- Designrr—This is a tool that will help you create ebooks from your published content such as blogs, audio, video, YouTube files, or previously published PDFs.

- Outgrow—Outgrow provides you with interactive lead magnets you can easily customize. The lead magnet templates they have include calculators, quizzes, assessments, surveys, and polls.

- Interact—Similar to Outgrow, but they only do one lead magnet and they do it well: quizzes.

Lead Magnet Promotion Tools

Many email marketing software solutions, like the one I use, ConvertKit, also include support for lead magnet promotion through landing page and pop-up builders. However, you might want to have a distinct look, feel, or more robust analytics and use a different tool for this.

- LeadPages—This tool began as a custom landing page building tool but now also includes pop-up forms and alert bars.

- OptinMonster—While OptinMonster does not offer landing pages, it offers every other conceivable way of displaying a lead magnet on your website, including gamified wheels. Also includes robust functionality, such as page level and geolocation targeting, exit intent detection, and over 100 templates to use.

- Sleeknote—An advanced pop-up builder with over 100 (!) email marketing software integrations that, besides pop-ups, also supports embeddable forms, sidebars, slide-ins, and gamification.

- Poptin—This is another advanced pop-up builder with dozens of integrations and features a variety of pop-ups including lightbox, gamified, countdown, slide-in, and top and bottom bar. It also has advanced targeting and trigger options together with A/B testing.

- OptimizePress—While only for WordPress users, it is a WordPress native plugin that allows you to create highly converting landing pages and inline forms.

Email Marketing Software

There is a plethora of email marketing software solutions that both integrate with the previous lead magnet distribution tools and offer their own solutions. Some of these solutions feature more marketing automation than others, and CRM functionality is usually another differentiator. These include:

- ActiveCampaign (B2B)
- Klaviyo (Ecommerce)
- Omnisend (Ecommerce)
- Mailchimp
- ConvertKit (currently using)
- MailerLite

Marketing Automation Software

Marketing automation software differs from email marketing software in that their focus is on lead generation, nurturing, and conversion over a longer sales cycle. Begin with one of the previous 6 email marketing software solutions—ActiveCampaign, Klaviyo, Omnisend, Mailchimp, ConvertKit, and MailerLite. When you see the ROI and/or are ready to invest in a high-end solution that focuses on marketing automation features, which are often tied to more of a CRM-based sales and marketing approach, then my recommendations would include:

- Hubspot
- Zoho Marketing Automation
- Keap (formerly known as InfusionSoft)
- Act-On

SOCIAL MEDIA TOOLS

Social Media AI Content Creation Tools

Most general AI tools support this, and you could even instruct ChatGPT and Google Gemini to do the same thing. These AI tools that have specific prompts for social media that I would recommend you check out would be:

- Jasper
- Tailwind Ghostwriter
- Copy.ai
- Rytr
- Anyword

Social Media Dashboards with Integrated AI Content Creation Tools

Optimize your workflow with AI tools that both help you create social media posts AND schedule them. These social media dashboards that also have integrated AI writers that I would recommend include:

- SocialBee
- Flick
- ContentStudio
- Ocoya
- Rapidely

Social Network-Specific AI Content Creation Tools

If you truly want to create platform authentic content, use the AI to analyze what types of posts are already doing well and then to introduce similar types of content or templates, If any of the following platforms are part of your Digital First strategy, I would definitely look into these tools:

- LinkedIn—Taplio
- Twitter—Tweet Hunter, Hypefury
- Pinterest—Pin Generator

User Generated Content

These platforms allow you to manage the entire lifecycle of user-generated content, which is to find, curate, manage, publish, and analyze its effectiveness. They also include an email component, which allows you to ask for reviews from your customers to encourage UGC submission, rights management for the UGC, and analytics to measure their ROI. These platforms include:

- Yotpo
- Tint
- Taggbox
- BazaarVoice
- FourSixty

Another type of platform does not help you source UGC from your fans but facilitates the creation of UGC on your behalf from their pool of content creators. You could consider them a UGC creator marketplace of sorts, each having a database of creators to choose from. This will cost you more than merely sending free product, but it is a type of influencer marketing that provides you tangible results in terms of content. These platforms include:

- Trend.io
- JoinBrands
- Insense
- Billo
- Collabstr

Another option to increase the creation of user-generated content around your brand is through a user-generated content giveaway encouraging people to submit photos and videos with branded hashtags. Here are some tools that can help you with this campaign, since not every contest or giveaway tools support contests that can generate user-generated content:

- Shortstack
- Gleam
- Woorise
- Woobox
- Viralsweep

Brand Ambassador

There are many influencer marketing and affiliate marketing platforms that also brand themselves as brand ambassador solutions. Make sure that they truly meet your needs as you are creating a program from people you already know. For this purpose, there are Shopify Collabs—free for Shopify customers, which includes an influencer database. The full list of recommended tools is:

- Shopify Collabs
- Refersion
- LeadDyno
- Influitive
- Brandbassador

External Influencer Search And Discovery

For influencer marketing and reaching out to external influencers, the tool is only the beginning. Make sure you analyze how each of these tools helps manage your lists, communication, and ultimately campaigns after you collaborate with them.

- Shopify Collabs—This is a straightforward decision if you have a Shopify store, however its influencer database might not be as comprehensive as some of the options below.

- Heepsy—Find Instagram and TikTok influencers with more than 5K followers, YouTube influencers with more than 1K subscribers, and Twitch streamers of all sizes.

- Influencity—Database has over 170 million influencers to search from.

- Modash—Their database has over 200 million influencers to search from.

- Inbeat—A spam-checked database with millions of Instagram and TikTok influencers.

For a B2B organization, or if you're looking to reach influential bloggers, these tools will help you find them:

- Buzzsumo
- Buzzstream
- Respona
- Ninja Outreach
- Pitchbox

PAID MEDIA

AI Tools to Generate Ad Copy

We covered some of these tools earlier, but these generative AI tools have specific functionality that helps you easily create ad copy:

- Jasper
- Copy.ai
- Writesonic
- Rytr
- Anyword

AI Tools to Generate Ad Creatives

Ads for social media often require visuals, both static and video, so we can use AI to create compelling ad creatives in a fraction of the time if used to take with the following tools to generate ad creatives.

Adobe Express—Includes all the templates, tools, and generative AI to create any creative that your heart desires easily.

AdCreative.ai—AI-generated creatives using an AI engine that is trained on data that converts to give your creatives an edge.

Creatopy—Create compelling video ads in minutes with this tool, their plethora of templates, and their ease of use. You can build ad designs across an extensive variety of sizes and formats.

Simplified—Allows you to create ads uniquely by first inputting your brand assets and then choosing your target audience and ad platforms. The AI Ads Generator will analyze your brand assets and target audience data to determine the best tone and length for the platform while focusing on your audience's challenges. Based on the analysis, the AI Ads Generator will generate the best-suited ad creative for your campaign, optimized for conversions.

Pencil—Helps you generate ad creatives predicted to win with AI.

General Ads Platform Tools

Although you can manage ads directly on the ad managers of each platform, there are a plethora of tools that allow you to manage your ads more efficiently across multiple networks on one platform. Some of these tools also include automation and AI technology for optimization.

AdRoll—This is an AI-centric ads management platform built for ecommerce that allows you to retarget and advertise on most of the digital platforms from one dashboard.

Adzooma—Helps manage ad campaigns on Google, Microsoft, and Meta and helps you improve your ads.

Optmyzr—Optmyzr contains everything you need to create, optimize, and justify high-performing PPC campaigns across Google and Microsoft. Includes a rule engine and customized recommendations.

Revealbot—Automated ad platform allowing you to optimize ad budget with automations, analyze, and launch improved ads. It supports Meta, Google, and Snap.

Madgicx—An AI-infused platform that has comprehensive functionality to handle complete and automated ad creative, ad management, targeting, and analytics. It supports Meta and Google Ads.

Amazon Ads Platforms

While there are several players in the space, I recommend you first investigate these tools if you are in ecommerce and advertising on Amazon:

- Helium 10
- SellerApp
- Perpetua

- SellerLabs
- Teikametrics
- Jungle Scout

NEW TOOLS, OLD RULES

Remember that the chapter on technology in *Digital Threads* was the final one. Some get caught up in the technology, but we say people, process, and tools in that order for a reason: A tool should only complement and not replace the Digital Threads processes you should have in place.

Good luck with your selection of tools from this glossary, and I would love to hear from you with your opinions on these tools or others that you might want to recommend for future inclusion here. You can contact me by email at neal@nealschaffer.com.

APPENDIX ON COMMON LEGAL ISSUES

With Digital Threads, there are a few areas where there are some legal issues that you must know when wading into these territories.

It surprises me how many brands are not aware of the FTC guidelines that govern influencer marketing. Similar email marketing and influencer marketing laws are emerging throughout the world. It is important to understand and follow these recommended methods to ensure legal compliance.

An important disclaimer: I am not, nor do I pretend to be, a lawyer. The following is not legal advice, only professional advice on legal issues related to some topics included in this book. If you are interested in learning more and/or implementing these legal guidelines in your company, please reach out to qualified and experienced legal help.

Email Marketing Laws

While there are other laws that exist regarding email communication, the CAN-SPAM act is the definitive one that says:

1. Your subscribers must have opted-in to receive a communication from you, and
2. You offer your subscribers a one-click unsubscribe option.

There are many that swear by cold outreach emails, a topic that I specifically did not cover in this book. This is when you normally buy a cold "list" and email thousands, if not tens of thousands of people with emails. This is a grey zone in that, should the email be relevant to that person—and the option exists to unsubscribe—these cold outreach emails aren't necessarily illegal. There is a burgeoning industry around them.

My advice, if you were to take this approach, is to purchase a domain that you will specifically use for your cold email outreach after you "warm up" this domain. Remember that you do not want to harm your relationship with the relevant email algorithms for your main business domain.

Influencer Marketing Laws

Influencer marketing is still a bit of the "wild west," but the laws are quickly playing catch up. It wasn't until 2023 that influencers had to say at the beginning of their TikTok video or podcast that the content was being sponsored. There have been some government lawsuits placed on influencers, but this history of FTC clampdowns shows that the burden falls on brands. If your influencers don't follow through on FTC guidelines, you, the business, could be at fault.

The FTC offers a free download to educate influencers on these guidelines in plain English (https://www.ftc.gov/system/files/documents/plain-language/1001a-influencer-guide-508_1.pdf). I would make sure that you include mention of FTC-compliance by the influencer in any contractual agreement with brand ambassadors or external influencers. The golden rule about being compliant is that the social media user must disclose the nature of the relationship with the sponsoring brand in a "clear and conspicuous" way. There are other guidelines, such as influencers must be truthful about their experiences with your products, but the important matter is that brand ambassadors will fall under the same category of coverage if you are giving them free product or somehow incentivizing them. The same goes for employees. Anytime there is a material relationship between the social media user and your company, the social media user MUST clarify it so that there is no potential for fake advertising. Remember: The FTC is there to protect the consumer and ensure fair competition.

For international brands, if some influencers you are engaging with have an audience in the United States, the FTC guidelines will apply to them, making it a current international standard.

There are other legal implications not covered here, such as GDPR privacy laws in Europe vis-à-vis your website and email marketing and the FTC clamping down on fake reviews, but I am assuming by now your business has already implemented and/or is aware of these.

Based on my experience, the email marketing and influencer marketing related issues are the ones that companies still fail to be 100% compliant with, thus this short appendix to help guide you and serve as an important reminder.

THANK YOU FOR READING
THE DIGITAL THREADS COMPANION WORKBOOK!

I appreciate any feedback and would love to hear what you thought about this workbook.

Your input is essential to help make this workbook and future books even better to serve more people.

Please take a minute now to leave a review on Amazon letting me know what you thought of the workbook:

nealschaffer.com/digitalthreadsworkbookreview

I cannot thank you enough! If you used a non-recognizable name, please send me a screenshot to neal@nealschaffer.com so that I can personally thank you!

Note that there is also a paperback version of this workbook that you can buy here:

nealschaffer.com/buydigitalthreadsworkbook

- Neal Schaffer

IF YOU LIKED DIGITAL THREADS, YOU'LL LIKE MY OTHER BOOKS:

nealschaffer.com/digitalthreads
The small business and entrepreneur
playbook for Digital First marketing.

nealschaffer.com/ageofinfluence
The definitive guide to influencer marketing.

nealschaffer.com/maximizeyoursocial
The definitive guide to creating and implementing a
social media marketing strategy.

nealschaffer.com/maximizinglinkedin
The definitive guide to using LinkedIn for social selling,
employee advocacy, and social media marketing.

Visit **nealschaffer.com/books/**
for more information.

WORK WITH ME

I work with businesses in a variety of ways, from strategy creation to audit, implementation to training. Please find more information below and contact me below if I can be of any help to you or your organization.

GROUP COACHING

My Digital First Mastermind Community includes four monthly Zoom calls, one quarterly 30-minute private coaching call, and a private Facebook Group.

PRIVATE COACHING

When you need one-on-one help. Provided in one-hour increments.

FRACTIONAL CMO

My signature marketing consulting service where I become your fractional CMO, and you leverage my expertise however you see fit. Flexible, cost-effective, and you retain all IP!

SPEAKING & TRAINING

Whether it is speaking at your event or hands-on training for your team, I can help.

nealschaffer.com/contact/

SUBSCRIBE TO MY NEWSLETTER

Every week I provide updates to my readers on the world of Digital Threads, including:

- **The latest digital marketing news**
- **Updates on search engine optimization**
- **Strategies for successful email marketing**
- **Trending topics in social media marketing**
- **The newest AI technologies and tips for marketing**
- **My latest YouTube video, podcast episode, and blog posts**

In addition, this is the best way to find out about my new books, speaking events, and free educational webinars and other resources that I provide!

Subscribe here:
nealschaffer.com/newsletter/

ABOUT THE AUTHOR

Neal Schaffer stands at the forefront of the digital marketing revolution, an innovative Fractional CMO and acclaimed authority whose insights and strategies have catalyzed the growth of businesses worldwide. With a career that spans over a decade and crosses four continents, Neal has solidified his reputation as a global thought leader in digital, content, influencer, and social media marketing.

Neal's passion for education and empowerment in the digital space comes to life through his roles as an instructor at prestigious institutions, including UCLA Extension and Rutgers Business School, where he covers crucial topics like personal branding, influencer marketing and social media branding. His commitment to nurturing the next generation of marketers extends beyond the classroom to the global stage, having delivered keynotes at hundreds of events worldwide.

Author of five pivotal sales and marketing books, Neal's publications such as *Maximize Your Social*, *The Age of Influence*, and his newest *Digital Threads* have been instrumental for professionals seeking to leverage the power of digital-first marketing. These works, acclaimed for their practical insights and forward-thinking strategies, underscore Neal's expertise and influence in the marketing domain.

Beyond his books, Neal enriches the digital marketing conversation with his Your Digital Marketing Coach podcast, offering weekly inspiration and actionable advice to help businesses and professionals stay ahead in the rapidly evolving landscape. Neal's blog at nealschaffer.com further establishes him as a leading resource, hosting hundreds of posts that serve as a vital toolkit for the business community.

With a storied career as a Fractional CMO and marketing consultant for an extensive array of brands, both large and small, Neal Schaffer's contributions to the marketing world are unmatched. His strategic vision, combined with a genuine dedication to empowering others, makes Neal Schaffer not just an expert in digital marketing, but a true pioneer reshaping the industry's future.